About Bee Bilingual

Bee Bilingual has been created by Madeleine, an experienced language teacher. She has worked in various settings, such as language schools and preschools, across the UK, Ireland and Germany. Because of the lack of English learning resources for children, Madeleine created this marvellous workbook. Visit **www.beebilingual.com** for more information.

CONTENT

6

www.beebilingual.org

FOREWORD

Children are interested in other languages and enjoy learning about other cultures and people. Therefore, a fun learning environment with interesting materials and activities is the key to a successful language learning experience. This workbook will provide you with various worksheets, ideas and much inspiration to guarantee that your children/students improve their English language skills.

Bee English Volume 1 **is suitable for absolute beginners** and **advanced students** from the reading age upwards. The exercises and corresponding pictures are designed to increase your children/students' vocabulary knowledge. Furthermore, the first sentence patterns and important grammatical aspects are introduced. By the end of this book, your child/student will have a language foundation with enough vocabulary to have basic conversations.

Teaching and learning a foreign language is like building a house. You need to have a solid foundation to build sturdy walls and a resilient roof. Similarly, every foreign language journey starts with a good foundation that consists of basic vocabulary, grammar and sentences. Just as a house must withstand thunderstorms, wind, the sun and heavy rain, knowing a foreign language can make children stronger and increase their confidence in every aspect of life.

Tips and tricks for parents and teachers

- Ensure that language learning is fun for your students/children. In this sense, 'play' should be an important part of your language sessions. Therefore, this workbook must be considered as an addition to songs, conversations and games.
- Too much pressure and too many expectations could reduce you children/students' interest. Focus on the positives and the achievements of your children/students.
- Collaboration plays an important part in language learning. An encouraging relationship between students and teacher or children and parent is especially important.
- Always remember: mistakes are a natural part of the language learning process. Keep your children/students motivated by giving positive encouragement.
- Repetition and revision are essential factors in language learning. New vocabulary and grammatical structures should be repeated briefly in every lesson.

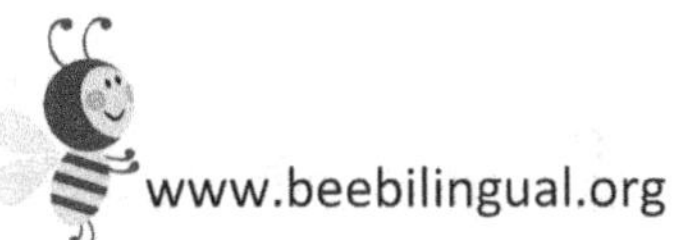

ACTIVITIES

- **Colourful, eye-catching displays:** Engaging displays can help children to memorise new vocabulary and grammatical structures. You can buy posters online or make your own. However, it is also important that children create their own displays. Provide the equipment and your knowledge and let your students work on their own posters.

- **Write your own lyrics:** You don't have to be a musician to co-write simple but effective lyrics with your students. You could start a lesson with a song that repeats words and basic English sentences from previous lessons.

- **Songs and rhymes:** If you are not too keen on writing your own songs, you could use YouTube as it is a great resource for English songs for children. New language patterns and vocabulary can be learned more easily with songs and rhymes.

- **Flashcards:** Flashcards are especially good for revising vocabulary in a fun way. They can also be used to play one of my favourite games called 'Memory', for which you simply need to use two sets of flashcards. This matching game and other memory and guessing games enable children to learn new vocabulary and sentences in an enjoyable way. As we all know, play is extremely important as it develops children's creativity and supports their brain development.

- **Drama activities:** Even if your students have limited language knowledge, drama activities can be especially useful. In my language lessons, my students like to pretend to go to a market to shop for vegetables and fruits. The contextual meaning helps the children to remember words and phrases. Furthermore, it increases students' motivation and interest in the English culture.

- **Guess the noun:** Another very popular game is 'Draw the noun', which is especially useful for reviewing vocabulary in a fun way. You could use flashcards as prompts; however, your students are not allowed to draw the image that is displayed on the flashcard. You could even ask your students to use full sentences, such as 'This is a book' instead of 'book' or 'the book'.

- **English folder:** Your students should have a folder for collecting worksheets, pictures and flashcards. It is a great way of gathering language knowledge and repeating words and structures that have already been learned.

Read and Learn

www.beebilingual.org

A. Draw matching pictures.

Good morning

Good day

Good evening

Good night

www.beebilingual.org

B. Translate the following expressions into your native language.

Hello ___________________

Thank you ___________________

You are welcome ___________________

Good morning ___________________

Please ___________________

Goodbye ___________________

Good evening ___________________

Good night ___________________

C. Translate the following sentences and question into your native language.

1. My name is... ____________________________

2. What's your name? __________________________

3. I'm fine, thank you. _______________________

4. How are you? ____________________________

6. I'm unwell. _____________________________

7. You are welcome. _________________________

www.beebilingual.org

WRITING

D. Copy the words, sentences and questions.

1. How are you?

2. Bye!

3. My name is...

4. Thank you!

5. Good morning!

6. Hello!

www.beebilingual.org

THAT'S ME!

E. Answer the questions.

1. How are you? I'm________________________, thank you.

2. What's your name? My name is ________________________.

I'm ________________________.

F. Draw your face. What can you say already?

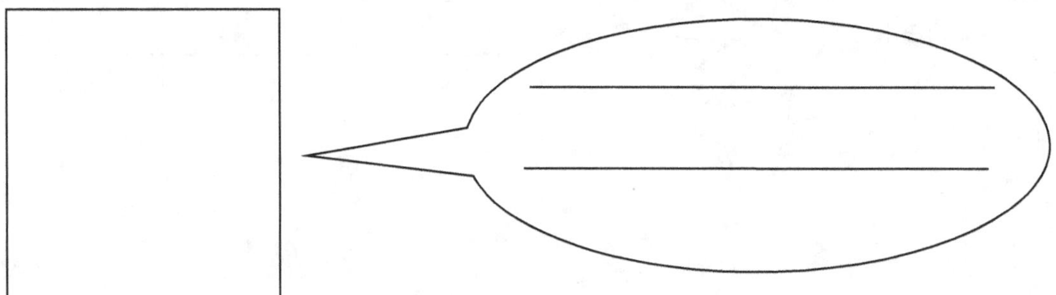

www.beebilingual.org

NAMES

G. Write sentences. Use 'My name is...' or 'I'm.....'.

www.beebilingual.org

Read and Learn

Numbers

1 - one
2 - two
3 - three
4 - four
5 - five
6 - six
7 - seven
8 - eight
9 - nine
10 - ten

A. Count the bears and birds. Write the number in the circle.

1 

2 

3 

4 

5

______
animals

6

______
bears

7

______
animals

8

______
birds

1 | One

3 |

5 |

6 |

10 |

2 |

WORD SEARCH

C. Find the numbers below in the grid.

- one 1   - five 5   - nine 9
- two 2   - six 6   - ten 10
- three 3   - seven 7
- four 4   - eight 8

O	A	B	T	E	N	V	I	E	R	N
N	T	Y	K	Z	K	S	I	X	G	I
E	C	Z	Y	E	A	N	E	U	N	N
S	S	A	C	T	W	O	L	E	F	E
F	D	O	K	H	M	D	C	H	D	B
Y	H	H	I	R	U	R	J	N	X	E
M	S	E	V	E	N	E	T	F	N	O
R	O	B	Z	E	E	I	U	O	E	G
F	K	V	H	F	K	R	K	U	U	H
E	I	G	H	T	J	O	I	R	F	B
F	I	V	E	S	H	M	P	N	F	R

HOW OLD ARE YOU?

D. How old are the children? Write sentences.

1. Peter, 9 years — PETER IS NINE YEARS OLD.

2. Emily, 8 years

3. John, 10 years

4. Olivia, 6 years

5. Emma, 7 years

And you? How old are you? You can also draw your face!

6. I'm _________________________.

www.beebilingual.org

Colours

B. Colour the balloons in the correct colour.

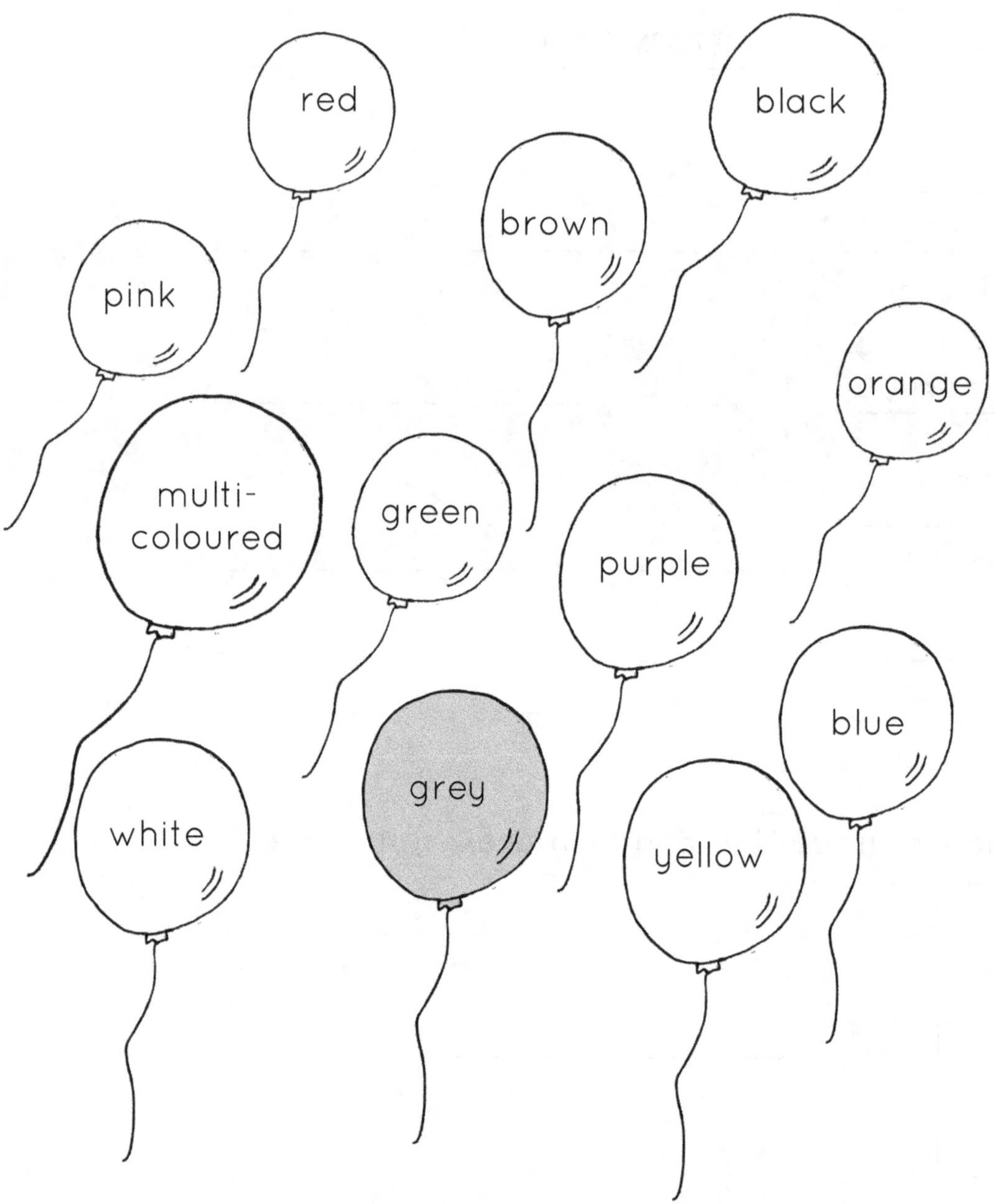

www.beebilingual.org

FRUITS AND VEGETABLES

A. Read and colour in the fruits and vegetables. Write the correct number in the circle.

1. Number one: the grapes are purple.
2. Number two: the lemon is yellow.
3. Number three: the orange is orange.
4. Number four: the carrot is orange.
5. Number five: the pepper is yellow.
6. Number six: the tomato is red.
7. Number seven: the cucumber is green.
8. Number eight: the apple is red.
9. Number nine: the banana is yellow.
10. Number ten: the pear is green.

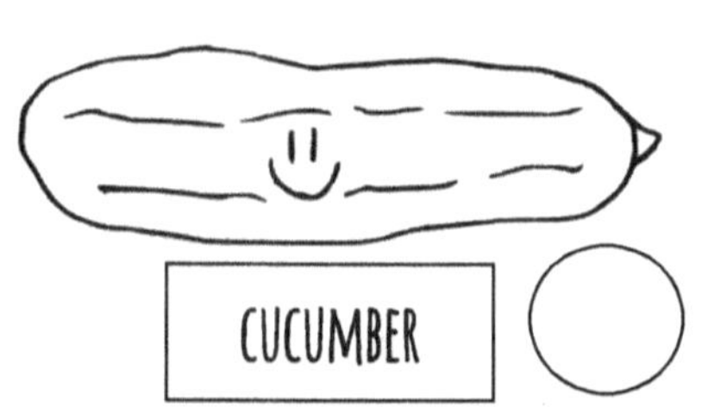

www.beebilingual.org

Carrot

1

PEPPER

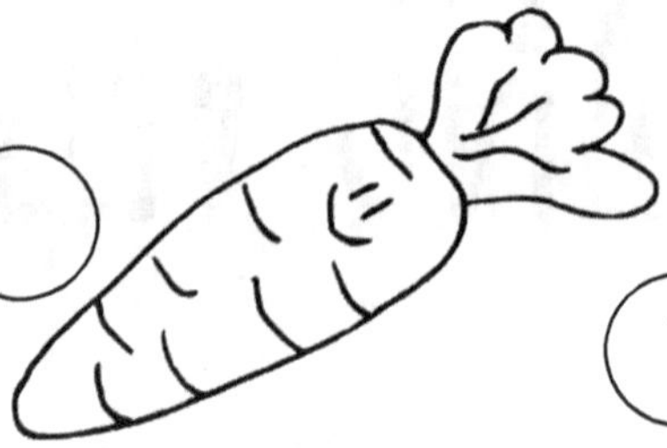

Grapes

Lemon

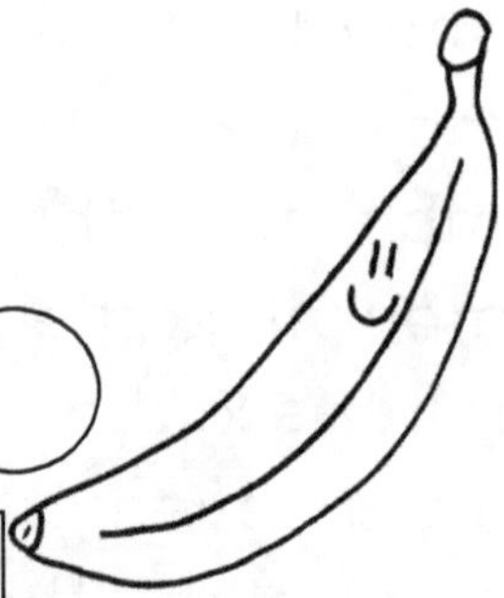

Banana

Tomato

Apple

I LIKE....

B. What fruits and what vegetables do you like/ do you not like?

1. Do you like pears?  YES, I LIKE PEARS. / NO, I DON'T/ DO NOT LIKE PEARS.

2. Do you like apples?  _______________________

3. Do you like carrots?  _______________________

4. Do you like tomatoes?  _______________________

5. Do you like bananas?  _______________________

6. Do you like lemons?  _______________________

7. Do you like oranges?  _______________________

www.beebilingual.org

DAYS OF THE WEEK

A. Find the days of the week in the grid. Then write the days of the week in the correct order.

- Monday   - Friday   - Saturday   - Sunday
- Wednesday   - Tuesday   - Thursday

MONDAY,____

M	O	N	D	A	Y	C	M	O	F	T
Z	W	S	U	N	D	A	Y	N	R	H
C	E	A	N	I	N	I	T	B	E	U
D	D	T	T	U	E	S	D	A	Y	R
M	N	U	T	W	O	C	H	B	T	S
B	E	R	S	S	J	S	I	D	A	D
W	E	D	N	E	S	D	A	Y	G	A
Y	B	A	S	A	F	R	I	D	A	Y
D	O	Y	N	E	R	S	T	A	G	I

Read and Learn

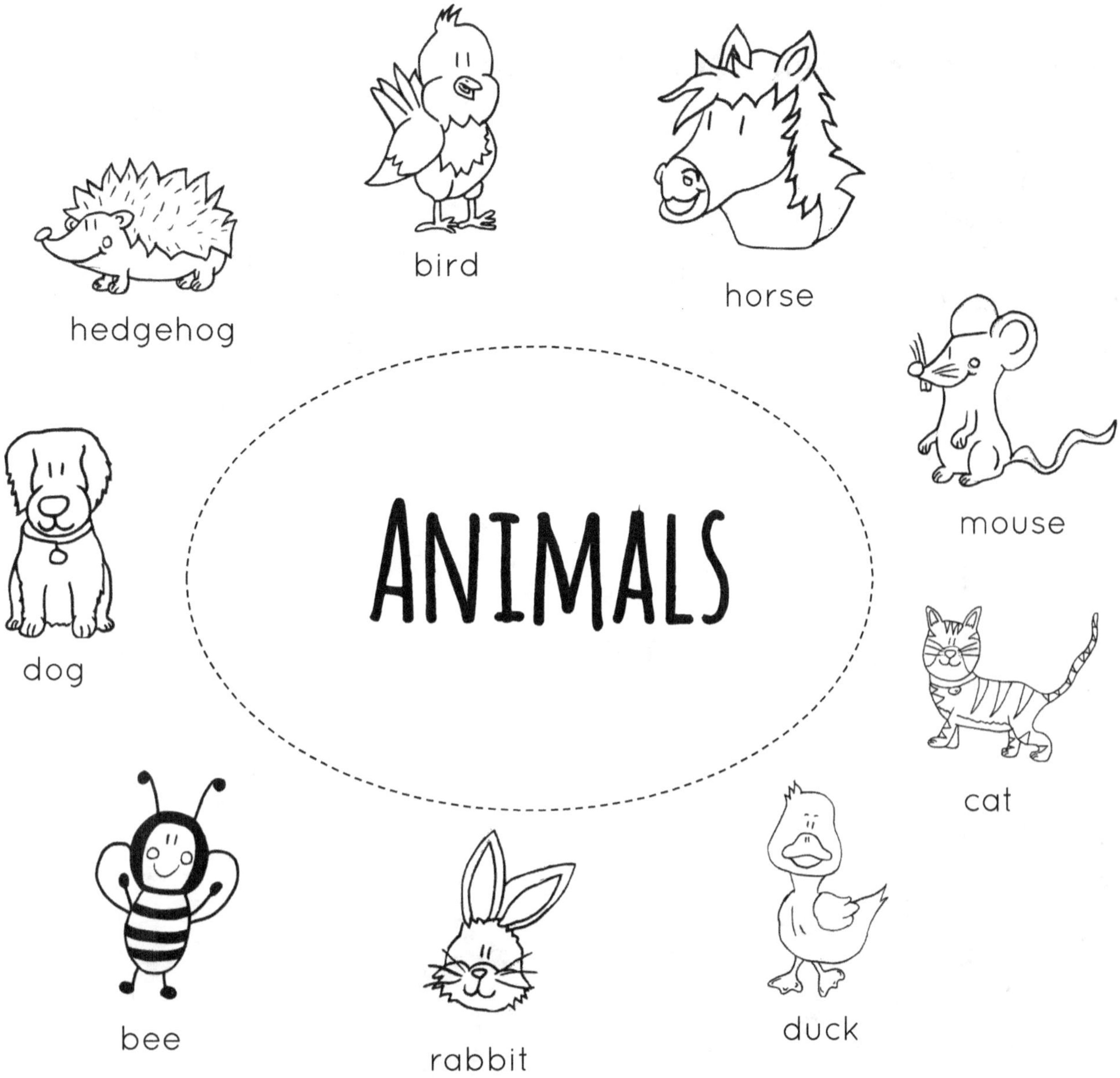

hedgehog

bird

horse

mouse

dog

ANIMALS

cat

bee

rabbit

duck

ANIMALS

A. Write the correct number in the circle.

(1)

1. dog

2. bird

3. cat

4. rabbit

5. horse

6. bee

7. hedgehog

8. mouse

9. duck

www.beebilingual.org

B. Complete the sentences. Use 'a'.

1. This is _A CAT._________________

2. This is _________________________________

3. This is _________________________________

4. This is _________________________________

5. This is _________________________________

6. This is _________________________________

7. This is _________________________________

8. This is _________________________________

9. This is _________________________________

www.beebilingual.org

READ AND LEARN

daughter/ sister

uncle

grandmother

cousin

FAMILY

aunt

father

son/ brother

grandfather

mother

FAMILY

A. Who is who? Fill in the words.

father	brother/ son	aunt	grandfather
mother	sister/ daughter	uncle	cousin

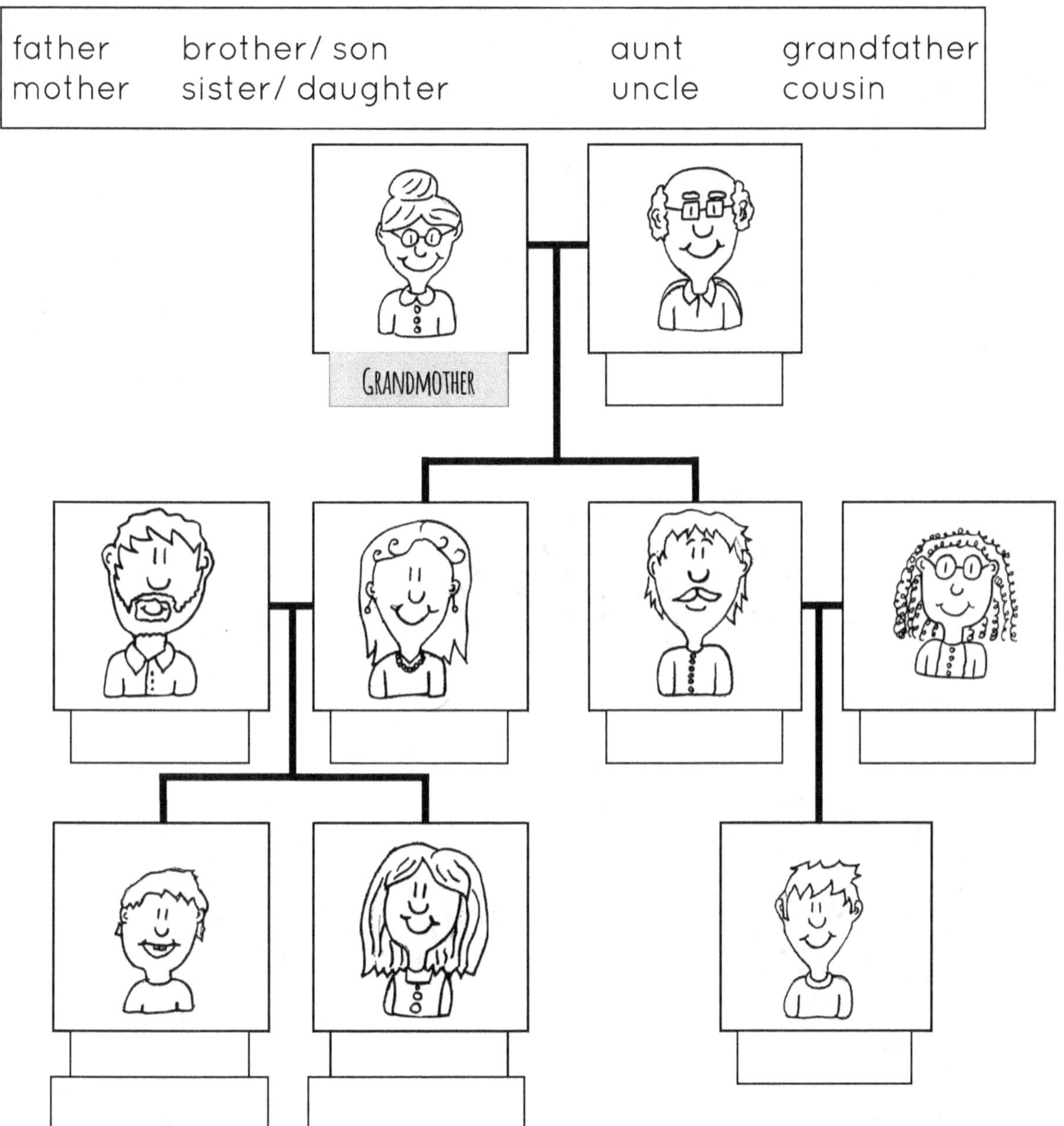

Read and Learn

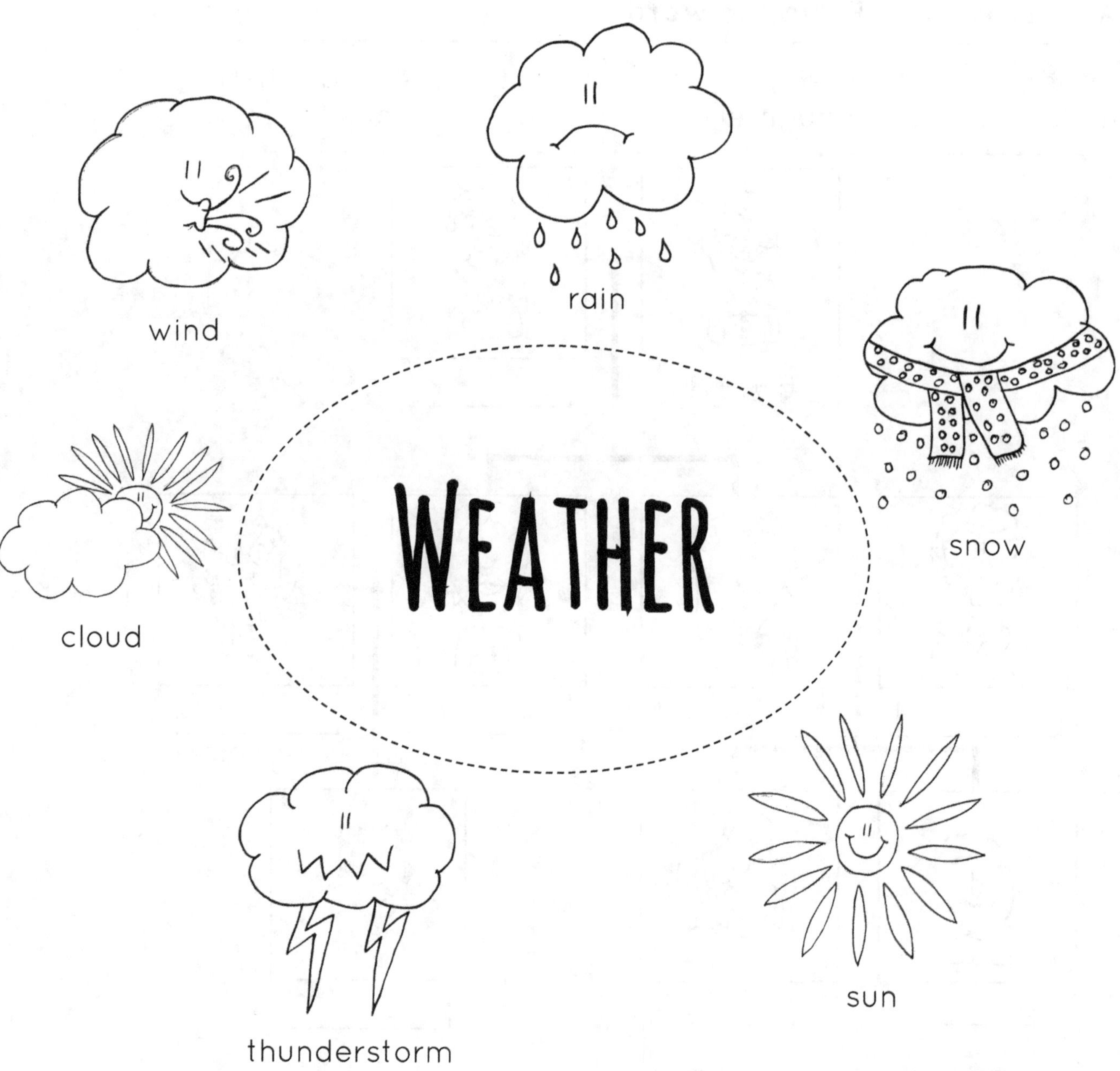

www.beebilingual.org

WEATHER

A. Match the words with the pictures and sentences.

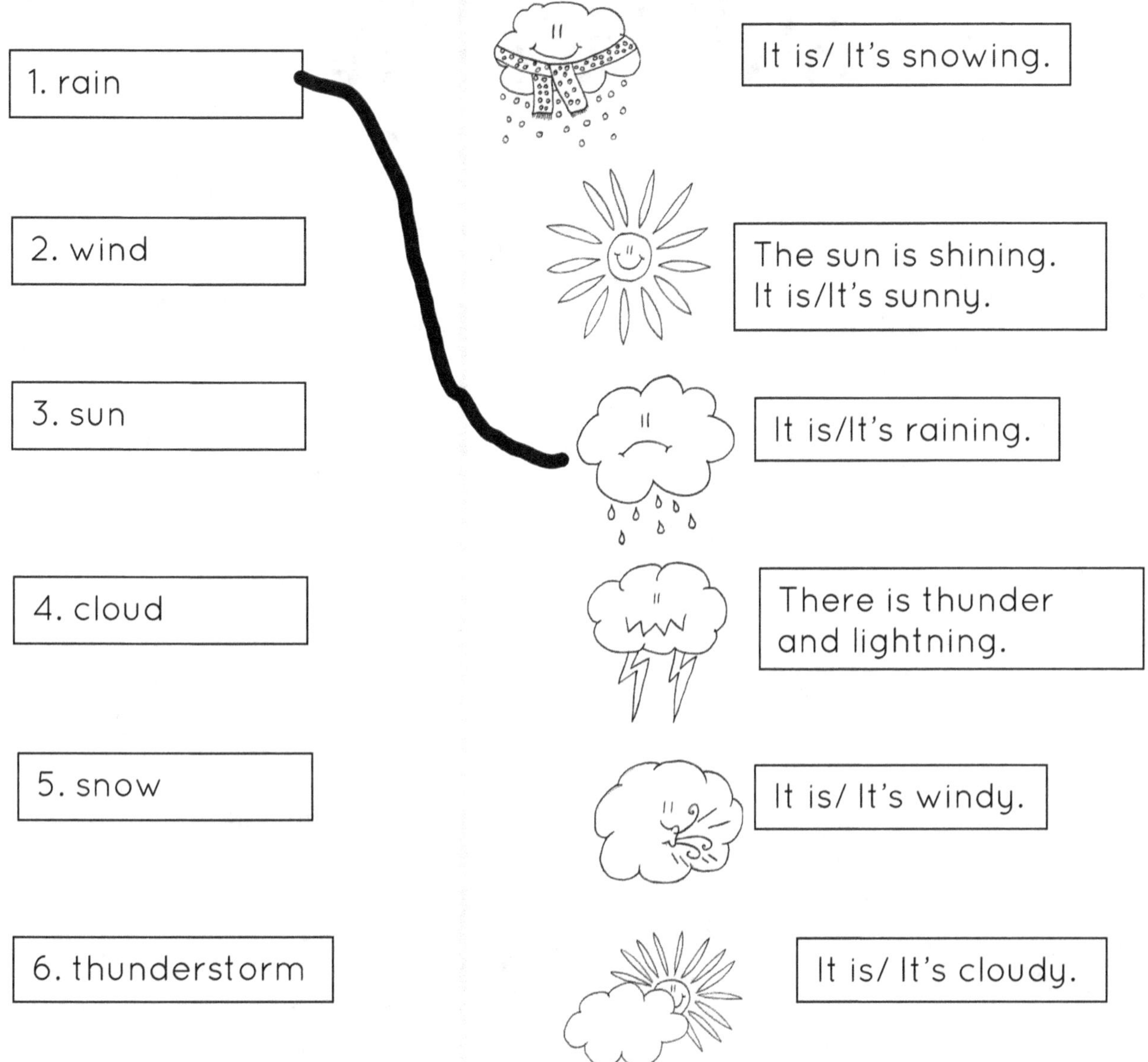

1. rain
2. wind
3. sun
4. cloud
5. snow
6. thunderstorm

It is/ It's snowing.

The sun is shining. It is/It's sunny.

It is/It's raining.

There is thunder and lightning.

It is/ It's windy.

It is/ It's cloudy.

www.beebilingual.org

MAP OF THE UNITED KINGDOM AND IRELAND

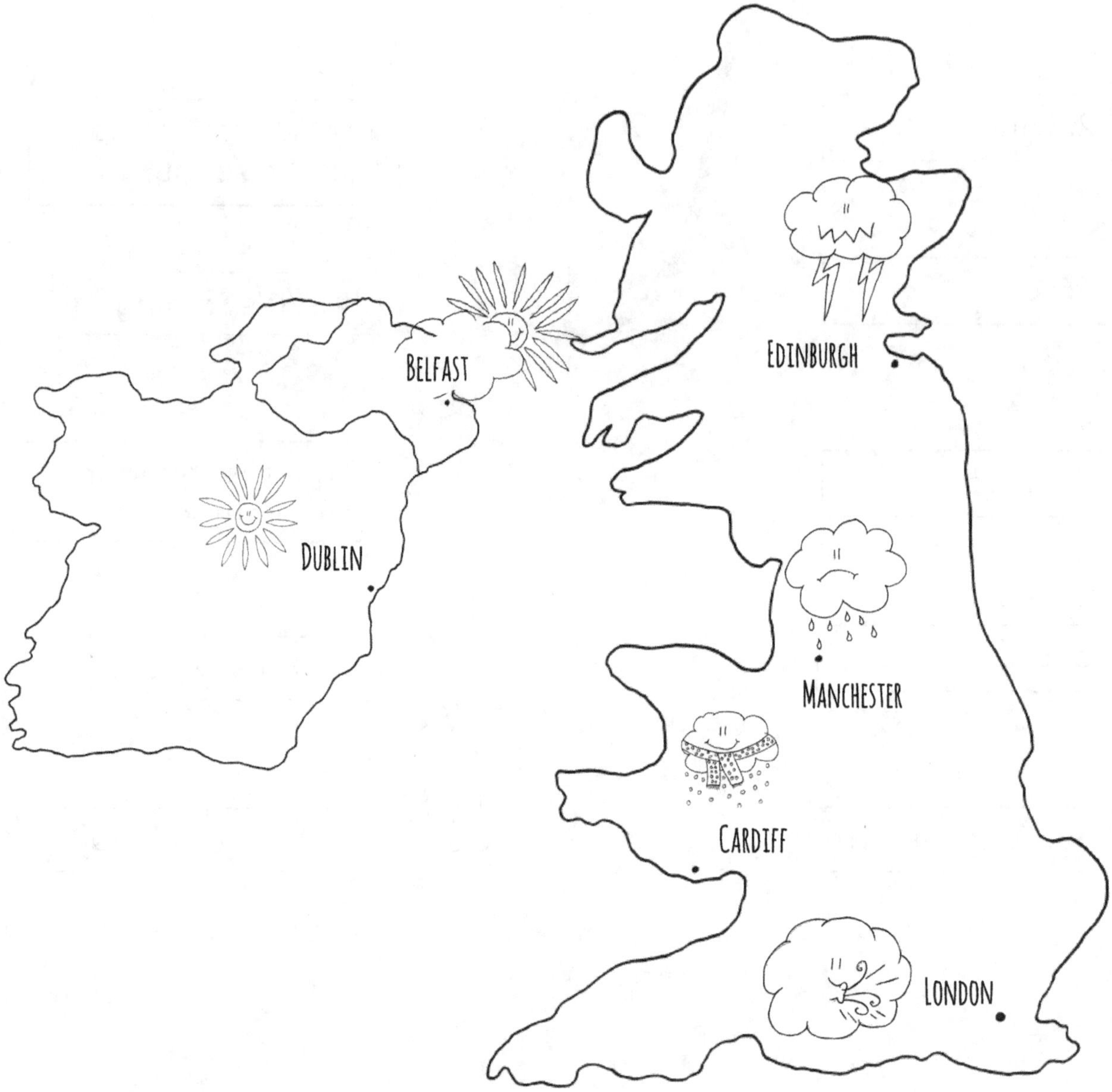

What's the Weather Like Today?

B. Look at the map. What's the weather like?

- It's raining.	- It's cloudy.	- The sun is shining.
- It's snowing.	- There is thunder and lightning.	

1. What's the weather like in London?

_______It's windy in London_______________________________________.

2. What's the weather like in Edinburgh?

____.

3. What's the weather like in Manchester?

____.

4. What's the weather like in Cardiff?

____.

5. What's the weather like in Dublin?

____.

6. What's the weather like in Belfast?

____.

Read And Learn

happy

sad

good/well

bad/unwell

Feelings

tired

angry

Draw the faces. How do the people feel?

happy

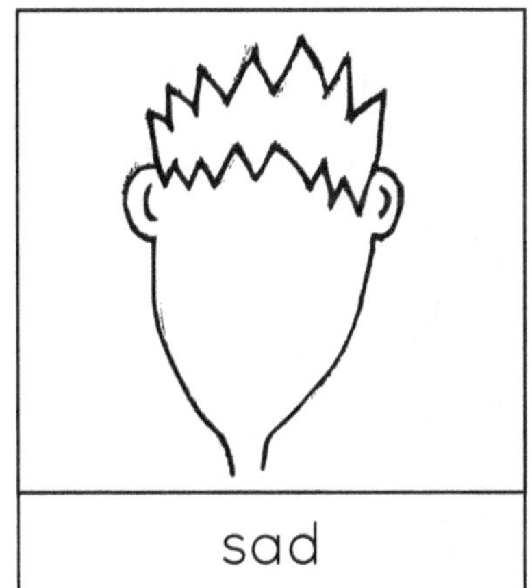

sad

angry

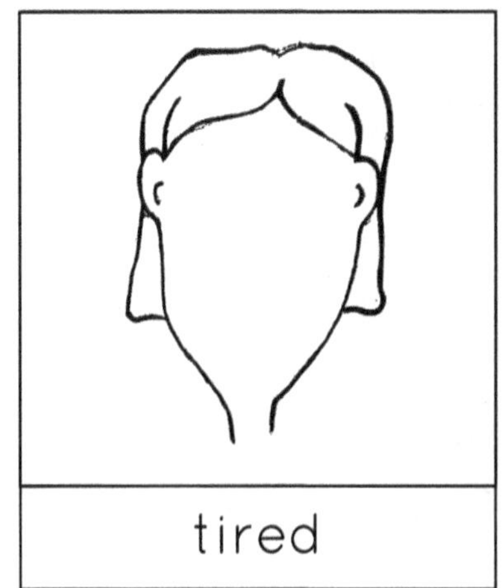

tired

good

bad

B. Finish the sentences.

well	tired
unwell	sad
angry	happy

1. 

I'm SAD. _______________________________

2. 

I'm _______________________________

3. 

I'm _______________________________

4. 

I'm _______________________________

5. 

I'm _______________________________

6. 

I'm _______________________________

READ AND LEARN

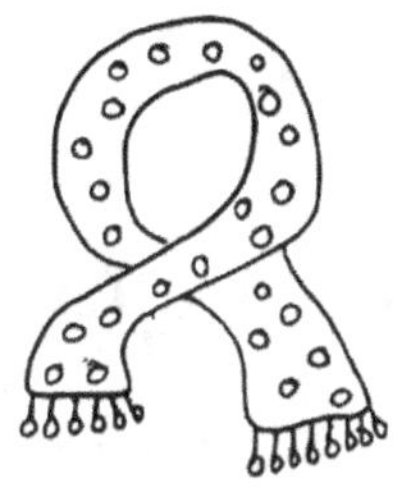
scarf

skirt

shorts

t-shirt

jumper

socks

Clothes

beanie

shoe

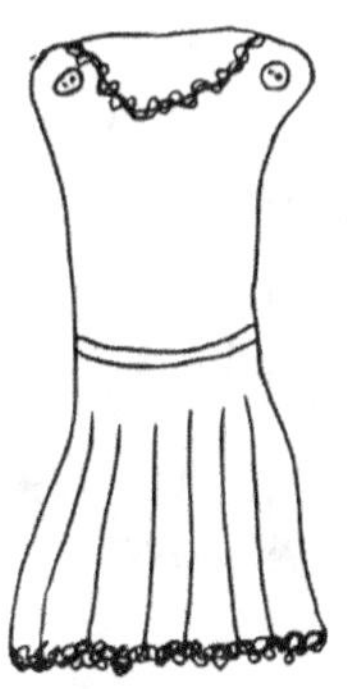
dress

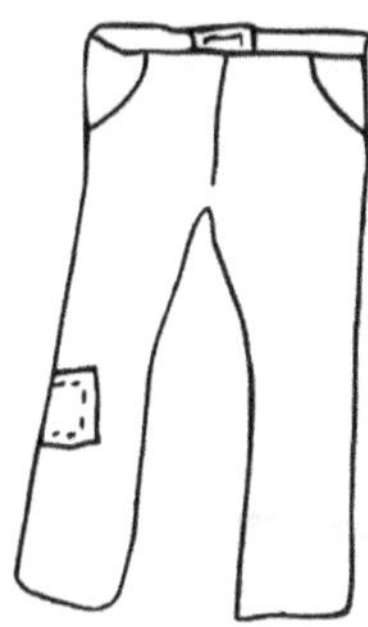
trousers

coat

www.beebilingual.org

Clothes

1. The **coat** is blue.
2. The **trousers** are brown.
3. The **scarf** is multi-coloured.
4. The **shoe** is black.
5. The **beanie** is yellow.
6. The **dress** is red.
7. The **shorts** are grey.
8. The **socks** are multi-coloured.
9. The **skirt** is green.
10. The **t-shirt** is pink.
11. The **jumper** is orange.

www.beebilingual.org

Read and Learn

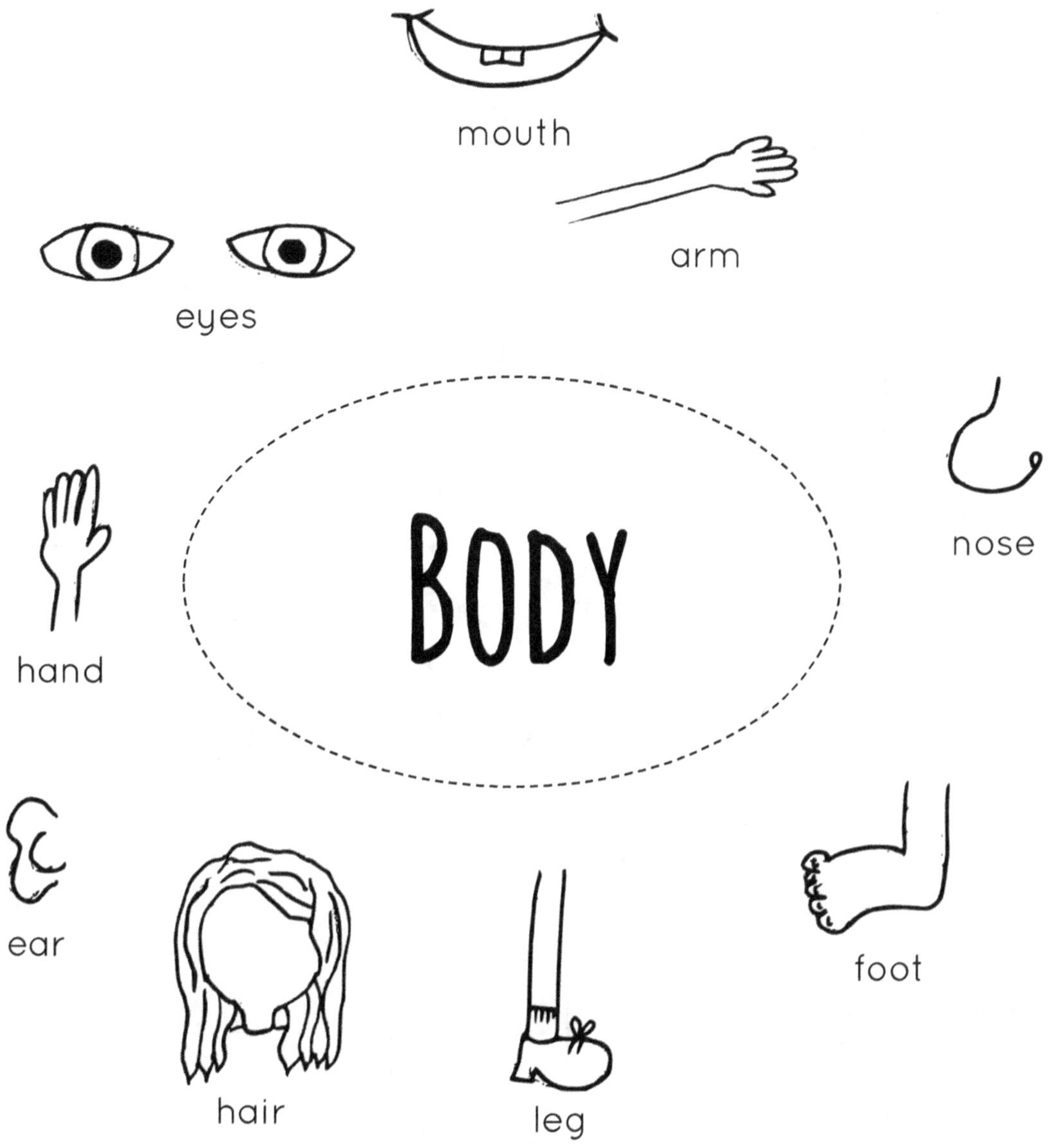

mouth

arm

eyes

Body

nose

hand

ear

hair

leg

foot

BODY

A. Match the words.

> ear   arm
> eyes   leg
> mouth   nose
> hand   hair
> foot

B. What are the parts of the body called? Write in the box.

1.

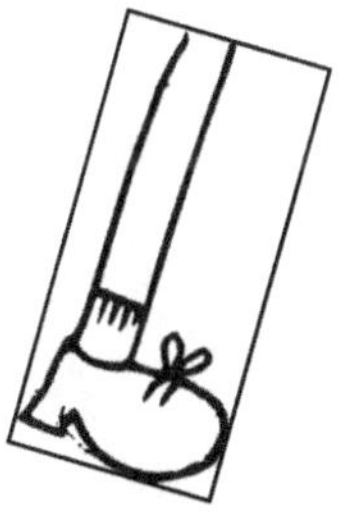

LEG

2.

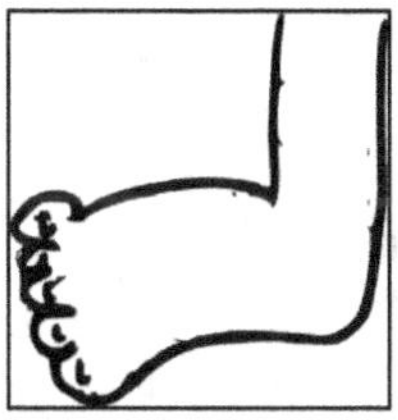

3.

4.

5.

6.

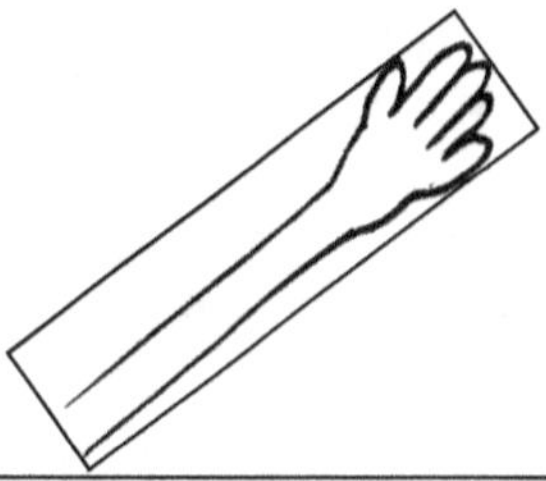

7.

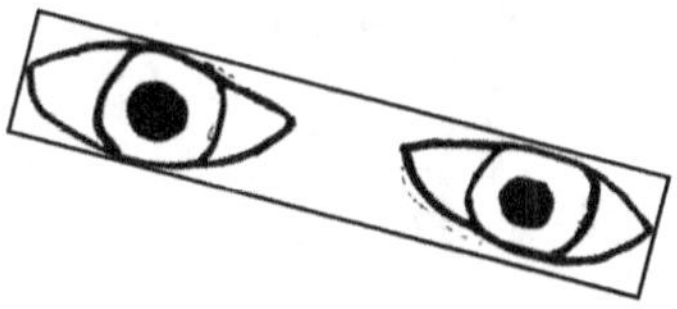

8.

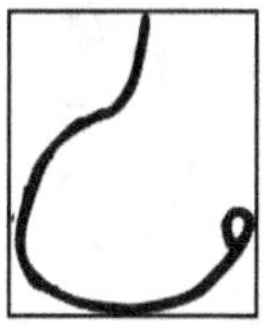

READ AND LEARN

to dance

to cycle

to play tennis

to play
football

Hobbies

to read

to shop

to sing

to swim

to listen to music

WHAT ARE YOUR HOBBIES?

A. Write the correct number in the circle.

1. singing
2. reading
3. playing football
4. dancing
5. shopping
6. listening to music
7. swimming
8. cycling
9. playing tennis

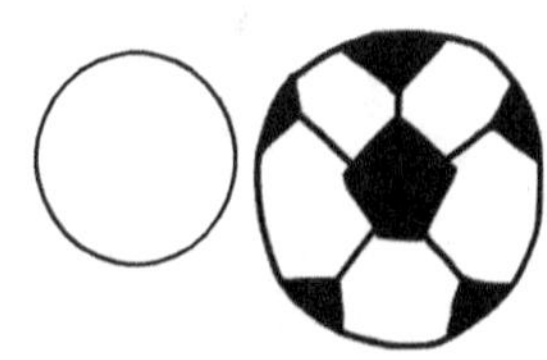

BᕗbW(Aᵗqbᴴ qbᴼz((qo+bᵈ q(n bᴿz(x)bАy bᴴ qbs m&)>

<table>
<tr><td>singing</td><td>cycling</td><td>dancing</td></tr>
<tr><td>playing football</td><td>playing tennis</td><td></td></tr>
<tr><td>reading</td><td>shopping</td><td></td></tr>
<tr><td>swimming</td><td>listening to music</td><td></td></tr>
</table>

1. Andrea's hobby **is** <u>SINGING</u>.

2. Alex's hobby **is**______________________________.

3. Daisy's hobby **is** _____________________________.

4. Andrew's hobby **is** _____________________________.

5. Heidi's hobby **is**______________________________.

6. Caroline's hobbies **are**___________________ and
_____________________.

7. Claire's hobbies **are** __________________ and
_____________________.

www.beebilingual.org

PROFILES

C. Read the following profiles. Then write your own profile and draw your face.

- WHAT'S YOUR NAME?

My name is Robert Williams.

- HOW OLD ARE YOU?

I'm eight years old.

- HOW ARE YOU?

I'm fine, thank you.

- WHAT ARE YOUR HOBBIES?

My hobbies are swimming and reading.

- WHAT'S YOUR NAME?

I'm Emma Smith.

- HOW OLD ARE YOU?

I'm seven years old.

- HOW ARE YOU?

I'm well, thank you.

- WHAT ARE YOUR HOBBIES?

Reading and cycling.

www.beebilingual.org

THAT'S ME 2

WHAT'S YOUR NAME?

____.

HOW OLD ARE YOU?

____.

HOW ARE YOU?

____.

WHAT ARE YOUR HOBBIES?

____.

ANSWERS

How old are you?
D. p. 17
Emily is eight years old.
John is ten years old.
Olivia is six years old.
Emma is seven years old.

I like...
B. p.21
2. Yes, I like apples. / No, I don't/ do not like apples.
3. Yes, I like carrots./ No, I don't like carrots.
4. Yes, I like tomatoes./ No, I don't like tomatoes.
5. Yes, I like bananas./ No, I don't like bananas.
6. Yes, I like lemons./ No, I don't like lemons.
7. Yes, I like oranges./ No, I don't like oranges.

Days of the week
A. p.22
Monday, Tuesday, Wednesday, Thursday, Friday, Saturday,
Sunday.

Animals
B. p.25
2. This is a hedgehog.
3. This is a dog.
4. This is a rabbit.
5. This is a bee.
6. This is a duck.
7. This is a mouse.
8. This is a horse.
9. This is a bird.

Weather
A. p.29
1. rain – It is raining.
2. wind – It is windy.
3. sun- The sun is shining.
4. cloud – It is cloudy.
5. snow – I is snowing.
6. thunder- It is thundering.

Feelings
B. p.34
2. I'm sad.
3. I'm happy.
4. I'm unwell.
5. I'm tired.
6. I'm angry.

What's the weather like today?
B. p.31
2. It's windy in London.
3. There is thunder and lightening
in Edinburgh.
4. It's snowing in Cardiff.
5. The sun is shining in Dublin.
6. It's cloudy in Belfast.

Body
B. p.39
1. leg
2. foot
3. hand
4. mouth
5. ear
6. arm
7. eyes
8. nose

Hobbies
B. p.42
2. Alex's hobby is playing football.
3. Daisy's hobby is listening to music.
4. Andrew's hobby is cycling.
5. Heidi's hobby is playing tennis.
6. Caroline's hobbies are reading and shopping.
7. Claire's hobbies are swimming and dancing.

www.beebilingual.org